The Green Roads

Illustrated by DIANA BLOOMFIELD

Holt, Rinehart and Winston

New York : Chicago : San Francisco

The Green Roads

Poems by EDWARD THOMAS, *1878 - 1917*

Chosen and with an Introduction

by ELEANOR FARJEON, *1881 - 1965*

PR
6039
.H55
Z7
1965

For Edward Thomas's Children
Mervyn, Bronwen and Myfanway (Ann)
and for Their Children
and Theirs

Walking with Edward Thomas

TO WALK WITH EDWARD THOMAS in any countryside was to see, hear, smell and know it with fresh senses. He was as alert to what was happening in and on the earth and the air above it as is an animal in the grass or a bird on a tree. Just as certain friends who share their thoughts with you will sharpen your thinking, he had the effect, when you took the road together, of quickening your seeing and hearing through his own keen eyes and ears. You would not

7

walk that road again as you did before. You would know it in a new way.

He himself was difficult to know. He was a man of moods, and whether he was happy or melancholy he withheld himself. While he shared with you his knowledge of the things that meant most to him, his self-knowledge was what he did not share. He reserved this as a deep pool hides a secret under the surface that reflects clearly every image and movement passing over it. To go for a walk with Edward Thomas was a sure way of discovering something you hadn't noticed about a tree, a weed, a flower, some difference in the sweet or acid notes in birds, how dry earth smells in spring, crumbles darkly in autumn, its freckled look under thaw, the feel of the sun on a stone or on your skin, the weather's changes of mood all the year round. It was also a way of discovering for yourself a little more of the man whose changes of humour resembled those of the weather, while he was talking of what he deeply loved. He loved equally all things natural, the acid sound and the sweet, the sour smell and the fragrant; the small white violets under the spring hedge, and the snow-white droppings of small birds on the hedge-leaves, were both dear to him. Still more he loved the traditions of the earth you were treading together; the past of the ancient earth of Kent and Wiltshire, or of his native Wales, which he loved better still. Best of all he loved the poets who made their poetry out of these things. On them he threw a light; he threw none on himself, until he also began to make poetry out of what he loved, two years before he died. How this happened through his friendship with Robert Frost is now so well-known to readers of modern poetry that it might seem unnecessary to tell it again. But no account of either of these men is complete without it.

Before they met, Edward Thomas confined himself to writing prose. He had always loved poetry beyond everything else, and in his boyhood attempted to write it and failed. Yet no man living understood more of the nature of poetry than he did, could recognise more quickly the real thing when he found it in a poem, or discard the poem that was sham and pretentious. He became one of the foremost critics of his time; a new poet could be made or undone by what he said. He had to struggle to keep his family, for reviewing is poorly-paid, and the books of fine prose which resulted from his walks all over England did not sell well. They continued to be published however because, without making money, he made a reputation which gave his name value to a publisher's list. Now the name has its sure place among English poets. He never dreamed it would be so, for he did not live to see his poems in print.

Forty-eight years have passed since he died, and today's young generation of readers may know his poems through modern anthologies, and in England hear his name often on the radio when poetry is read and poets talked about; his indissoluble link with Robert Frost, who lost his dearest friend when Edward died, is known in both England and America. In 1917 these two were contemporaries; now the half-century that divides them cannot separate them. But Frost was living and world-famous when the present generation was being born, and his recent death has not put him in the past. It is for the young, to whom Edward Thomas has never been a living personality, that this collection of his poems has been chosen. For them, too, it may be as well to set up a few signposts on the road.

Edward Thomas was born in Lambeth on the Third of March, 1878, and he was educated at St. Paul's School. But he cannot be thought of as a townsman. His parents came from Wales, and the mystery of all things Welsh was in his blood. He spent his holidays in the country, fishing, birdnesting, walking and reading, and spent his money on books of the open air: books by field naturalists like Richard Jefferies, by men like George Borrow and Giraldus Cambrensis who tramped England and Wales, cramming notebooks with their lore and curiosities—above all, he filled his bookshelves with the poets. Wherever he went he too crammed notebooks with anything that seemed to him worth noting, and began to write in earnest at sixteen, hardly allowing a week to pass, he said, "without writing one or two descriptions—of a man, or a place, or a walk."

Some of these essays appeared in weekly papers, through the help of James Ashcroft Noble, a well-known writer who believed in this young man. So did Helen, James Ashcroft's second daughter. *The Woodland Life,* Edward's first book of prose, appeared when he was nineteen. At the same age he won an Exhibition to Oxford. He married Helen Noble before he took his degree, and afterwards they made their first home in Kent, Helen's love of the country being as great as his. None of their married life was lived in a town. Their three children were country-born and bred, and bore Welsh names from the legends Edward loved: Merfyn, Bronwen, Myfanwy. Their cottage life was natural, simple, and economical. They were poor, but the air in the home was rich with what money can't buy. The work in the garden was shared, and Helen made cheerful use of every scrap of produce in its season. No meals tasted better than her home-baked ones; home-making for her family was her happiness, shadowed only by Edward's fits of depression and irritability. He went regularly to London to see editors and publishers, and meet his circle of literary friends; then, a new job in hand, would be off for several weeks on one of the walks that provided material for another book. For him walking and working went together. His long legs and his hawk's eyes were part of his stock-in-trade; so were the large maps he walked by, finding his way up hill and down dale by the contour-shading where no footpaths were marked; so too was the strong stick that companioned his stride, cut by himself from any hedge-tree—holly, hazel, ash or oak—in which he espied a straight limb for a staff; so was the pipe he smoked to companion his thoughts—a thick-stemmed clay, coloured by long smoking. His deep-set blue eyes changed to grey or darkened according to the weather in himself; the sun seemed to gild the colour of his cheeks, and glinted in his tawny hair. His gait when he walked was easy, never hurried. He had physical beauty which his friends described as faun-like, and his grave-toned voice was beautiful, talking or singing. The Thomas home-life embraced songs and music as well as tales and rhymes: rollicking sea-shanties, haunting folk-tunes, sweetest of all the songs of Wales sung in Welsh by Edward bathing and towelling the baby before the living-room fire, while in the kitchen Helen prepared her soups and puddings for supper. The two elder children were day-scholars at a famous co-educational school near by; at home Helen and Edward gave them the education school can't supply or supplant. They learned as they walked with Edward not knowing how much they were learning. The poems he wrote for each of his children are in this book.

He had not written them when, in 1913, I came to know the family, and stayed often in the workman's cottage in Hampshire. On one of my earliest visits Edward gave me a copy of his *Light and Twilight*. I knew his work as a reviewer, but nothing at that time of his own prose writings. When the children had gone to bed, Helen and he and I sat on, drinking tea and talking; and presently he read aloud to us. Poetry of course, from the new books sent him for review. Walter de la Mare's *Peacock Pie*, Ralph Hodgson's *Eve*, and W. H. Davies's *Foliage* had all been published that summer. Was one of the poems we listened to that night "A Greeting" from *Foliage?*

> Good morning, Life—and all
> Things glad and beautiful.
> My pockets nothing hold,
> But he that owns the gold,
> The Sun, is my great friend—
> His spending has no end.

I would like to think he read this, because Edward's great love of the sun was one day to find full expression in a poem; and it filled my first taste of his prose when I went up to bed that night and read the opening paragraph of *Light and Twilight*.

So strong was the young beauty of the year, it might have seemed at its height were it not that each day it grew stronger. The new day excelled the one that was past, only to be outshone by the next. Day after day the sun poured out a great light and heat and joy over the earth and delicately-clouded sky. The south wind flowed in a river from the sun itself, and divided the fresh leaves with never-ceasing noise of amorous and joyful motion. So mighty was the sun that the miles of pale new foliage shimmered mistily like snow, yet each leaf was cool and moist with youth, and the voices of the birds creeping and fluttering among the branches were as the souls of that coolness and moistness and youth. If one moment the myriad forms of life and happiness intoxicated the delighted senses, at another a glimpse of the broad mild land stretched out below, and of the sun ruling it in the blue above, gave also a calm and a celestial dignity and simplicity to the whole. One after another the pools, the rivers and rivulets, the windows or glass roofs of the vale, caught the sun and sparkled as if Vega and Gemma and Arcturus and Sirius and Aldebaran and Algol had fallen among the meadows and the woods.

Next day when we met at breakfast (he and Helen had been up long before me, doing indoor and outdoor chores, while I lay in bed making friends with little Myfanwy, who was then always called Baba and now is always called Ann), I asked him, "Have you ever written poetry, Edward?"

"Me? I couldn't write a poem to save my life."

But *Light and Twilight* teemed, I thought, with poetry. Another year was to pass before Robert Frost, having read *Light and Twilight* and *The South Country,* told his friend, "You've been writing as good poetry as any man living, and didn't know it."

Frost had been writing poetry for more than twenty years when the two men met; one a born poet, although as yet unpublished, the other a poet waiting to be born. Both poor, both having to reckon every penny, both with families. Robert had brought his to England hoping to find better fortune than in America. He found, if not fortune, at least a publisher for his first two books, and the books found him friends among the English poets. To Edward, *North of Boston* was the biggest experience in his years of reviewing. He helped to bring the unknown poet into prominence. This was a new tone in poetry. The American used no grandeur of language, no mighty rhythms, no lyrical charm; for what he had to say he used the natural cadence of the human voice. A poem by Robert Frost cannot be "recited" or declaimed or intoned, it has to be spoken. Frost detected a similar cadence in Edward's prose; it could become his medium for poetry. They discussed it endlessly, they could not see enough of each other, they pursued poetry when they walked, when they ate, when they sat up late in one of their homes or the other. Frost had made a new mode in poetry his own; but poetry has changed its mode from century to century, since poets first began to write in English. Edward knew every mode that had produced the great poems he admired and loved, but he could have used none of them naturally. Suddenly, startlingly, here was one he could use. The pent-up pool found an outlet, and became a flood. In September 1914 he wrote his first poem. Now he hastened every day to his study on the hill, to review other men's poetry because he had to, and pour out his own because he couldn't help it. He could hardly wait, he wrote, to light his fire before he began. "It has perhaps become a really bad habit." From March 1915 it was almost as though he were writing against time.

The dark moods that had tormented him lightened with this release into self-expression. It may have been a greater sureness of himself that led him to decide to join the army. In July 1915 he became a soldier. He need not have done so, or after his training have gone on active service. He did not love war, he did not hate the Germans; when asked what he was fighting for, he crumbled a handful of English earth between his fingers and said, "Literally for this." I think he also needed to prove himself in more new ways than one; he wanted to know that he was not afraid to face what other men were facing. In January 1917, with Frost's third book of poems in his haversack, he sailed for France, and had his thirty-ninth birthday there on March the Third. During that month, while he was preparing for his first battle, he was testing his courage. He wrote to Robert, now in America, where Edward hoped to join him after the war, that "he hadn't been given anything yet he couldn't do." His first and last battle was fought on the field of Arras on April 9; it was an Easter Monday. The day had been a triumph for his battery. While the English soldiers shouted and danced on the field, he left the dug-out behind the gun he had charge of, and began to stuff his clay pipe for a smoke. It was half filled when a stray bomb from the retreating Germans came over. The blast took him. He fell, knowing nothing. His pipe was un-broken.

In my arrangement of these poems I have begun with a main group of those which a companion might have shared who walked with Edward Thomas in different places at different times of the year. In them he does not give you birds and trees, woods, water and weather, as though they were a part of himself; he describes them in their own right, as he sees them. But while he is doing so, he becomes a part of them. This is the paradox, the secret of the pool, whose surface reflects what is outside itself, and under the surface is one with the reflection. He came near to explaining this paradox in a letter he wrote after he had sent me a poem that is not in this book.

"I am glad you liked the Sedge-warblers. Of course if I could really bring things pure and clear through verse into people's heads it would be a great thing. I rather fancy you doubt if it would necessarily be poetry. Well, I don't know either and I am not sure that I care. I am not trying to do anything in particular but only hoping that I have stepped into the nearest approach I ever made yet to self-expression."

Here is his description of the birds he had seen and heard on a lovely day in May:

> "sedge-warblers, clinging so light
> To willow twigs, sang longer than the lark,
> Quick, shrill, or grating, a song to match the heat
> Of the strong sun, nor less the water's cool,
> Gushing through narrows, swirling in the pool.
> Their song that lacks all words, all melody,
> All sweetness almost, was dearer then to me
> Than sweetest voice that sings in tune sweet words.
> This was the best of May—the small brown birds
> Wisely reiterating endlessly
> What no man learnt yet, in or out of school."

There is the sedge-warblers' song indeed "brought pure and clear into people's heads"; so different from the song of skylark, chaffinch or thrush that it is enough for us to know it by if ever we hear it sung among the sedge in May. And the paradox? He gives us the song-recording at the end of the poem; it begins with his dream of a beauty lovelier than the spring day which evokes it, a beauty that existed in a time "long past and irrecoverable . . . beauty divine and feminine, child to the sun." The longed-for beauty that only existed in legend in a time that never was. He sets them side by side in that May-day scene—the reality which meant so much to him, the unattainable dream which meant so much more. He knew that to attain it would be to lose it, that it could never equal his imagining. Again and again he haunts his poems with his longings. He is the aspen in the verse of that name, the ghost in "Two Pewits", the tench entangled in weeds on a day when his whole desire is for the sky, "nothing but sky".

Our walk with Edward Thomas ends with his second poem about roads. For now "all roads lead to France" he says in it, and in the small groups that follow he is alone: both in those in which the rhythms sing more lightly, as in the graver group where his moods are dissatisfied. I think some of these were written under the stress of indecision before he stepped firmly on the road that led to France, for in the last group, after the trumpet-call "Rise up! Rise up!" the poems express a new tranquillity. In "Lights Out", the last but one of these and to me the loveliest, he is a man who has shed everything and is preparing to go into the unknown where he must be uncompanioned. After this poem comes "In Memoriam, Easter 1915"; it was written for the men who had died in France before he himself was a soldier. But this is where it belongs, prophetic of himself two Easters later.

The last poem, different from everything else in the book, is the supremely beautiful "Words". It is the poet's appeal to the medium of all poets, that he may be chosen as their medium when, in the great experience that has come upon him, Edward Thomas was making "the nearest approach to self-expression I ever made".

If in this foreword I have stressed how much, except in his poems, he withheld himself from his friends, to one at least he gave himself unreservedly; the friend he walks with in the second poem in the book.

> The sun used to shine while we two walked
> Slowly together, paused and started
> Again, and sometimes mused, sometimes talked
> As either pleased, and cheerfully parted
>
> Each night. We never disagreed
> Which gate to rest on—

The friend of course was Robert Frost. "The Sun Used to Shine" is Edward's special poem for the man with whom he could talk, or not-talk, of anything and everything above and below the surface, with whom he could travel a road, or rest on it, as with nobody else. This poem says more than any other what walking with Edward Thomas could be when two are in perfect accord, as these two were; when the talk roved naturally from men and poetry to the wars of the present and past; when the silences fell easily on speech and thought, and their kindred senses absorbed the pallor of autumn crocus, the flavour of wasp-stung apples, the glitter of water in the moonlight. This was the poets' walk, taken when Edward Thomas was making England realise the poet in Robert Frost, and Robert was making Edward realise the poet in himself. These were the two friends' gifts to one another.

ELEANOR FARJEON

Contents

23

24

Two

Three

Four

26

One

One

The Green Roads

The green roads that end in the forest
Are strewn with white goose feathers this June,

Like marks left behind by someone gone to the forest
To show his track. But he has never come back.

Down each green road a cottage looks at the forest.
Round one the nettle towers; two are bathed in flowers.

An old man along the green road to the forest
Strays from one, from another a child alone.

In the thicket bordering the forest,
All day long a thrush twiddles his song.

It is old, but the trees are young in the forest,
All but one like a castle keep, in the middle deep.

That oak saw the ages pass in the forest:
They were a host, but their memories are lost,

For the tree is dead: all things forget the forest
Excepting perhaps me, when now I see

The old man, the child, the goose feathers at the edge of
the forest,
And hear all day long the thrush repeat his song.

The Sun Used to Shine

The sun used to shine while we two walked
Slowly together, paused and started
Again, and sometimes mused, sometimes talked
As either pleased, and cheerfully parted

Each night. We never disagreed
Which gate to rest on. The to be
And the late past we gave small heed.
We turned from men or poetry

To rumours of the war remote
Only till both stood disinclined
For aught but the yellow flavorous coat
Of an apple wasps had undermined;

Or a sentry of dark betonies,
The stateliest of small flowers on earth,
At the forest verge; or crocuses
Pale purple as if they had their birth

In sunless Hades fields. The war
Came back to mind with the moonrise
Which soldiers in the east afar
Beheld then. Nevertheless, our eyes

Could as well imagine the Crusades
Or Caesar's battles. Everything
To faintness like those rumours fades—
Like the brook's water glittering

Under the moonlight—like those walks
Now—like us two that took them, and
The fallen apples, all the talks
And silences—like memory's sand

When the tide covers it late or soon,
And other men through other flowers
In those fields under the same moon
Go talking and have easy hours.

Cock-Crow

Out of the wood of thoughts that grows by night
To be cut down by the sharp axe of light,—
Out of the night, two cocks together crow,
Cleaving the darkness with a silver blow:
And bright before my eyes twin trumpeters stand,
Heralds of splendour, one at either hand,
Each facing each as in a coat of arms:
The milkers lace their boots up at the farms.

If I Should Ever by Chance

If I should ever by chance grow rich
I'll buy Codham, Cockridden, and Childerditch,
Roses, Pyrgo, and Lapwater,
And let them all to my elder daughter.
The rent I shall ask of her will be only
Each year's first violets, white and lonely,
The first primroses and orchises—
She must find them before I do, that is.
But if she finds a blossom on furze
Without rent they shall all for ever be hers,
Whenever I am sufficiently rich:
Codham, Cockridden, and Childerditch,
Roses, Pyrgo and Lapwater,—
I shall give them all to my elder daughter.

What Shall I Give?

What shall I give my daughter the younger
More than will keep her from cold and hunger?
I shall not give her anything.
If she shared South Weald and Havering,
Their acres, the two brooks running between,
Paine's Brook and Weald Brook,
With pewit, woodpecker, swan, and rook,
She would be no richer than the queen
Who once on a time sat in Havering Bower
Alone, with the shadows, pleasure and power.
She could do no more with Samarcand,
Or the mountains of a mountain land
And its far white house above cottages
Like Venus above the Pleiades.
Her small hands I would not cumber
With so many acres and their lumber,
But leave her Steep and her own world
And her spectacled self with hair uncurled,
Wanting a thousand little things
That time without contentment brings.

If I were to Own

If I were to own this countryside
As far as a man in a day could ride,
And the Tyes were mine for giving or letting,—
Wingle Tye and Margaretting
Tye,—and Skreens, Gooshays, and Cockerells,
Shellow, Rochetts, Bandish, and Pickerells,
Martins, Lambkins, and Lillyputs,
Their copses, ponds, roads, and ruts,
Fields where plough-horses steam and plovers
Fling and whimper, hedges that lovers
Love, and orchards, shrubberies, walls
Where the sun untroubled by north wind falls,
And single trees where the thrush sings well
His proverbs untranslatable,
I would give them all to my son
If he would let me any one
For a song, a blackbird's song, at dawn.
He should have no more, till on my lawn
Never a one was left, because I
Had shot them to put them into a pie,—
His Essex blackbirds, every one,
And I was left old and alone.

Then unless I could pay, for rent, a song
As sweet as a blackbird's, and as long—
No more—he should have the house, not I
Margaretting or Wingle Tye,
Or it might be Skreens, Gooshays, or Cockerells,
Shellow, Rochetts, Bandish, or Pickerells,
Martins, Lambkins, or Lillyputs,
Should be his till the cart tracks had no ruts.

And You, Helen

And you, Helen, what should I give you?
So many things I would give you
Had I an infinite great store
Offered me and I stood before
To choose. I would give you youth,
All kinds of loveliness and truth,
A clear eye as good as mine,
Lands, waters, flowers, wine,
As many children as your heart
Might wish for, a far better art
Than mine can be, all you have lost
Upon the travelling waters tossed,
Or given to me. If I could choose
Freely in that great treasure-house
Anything from any shelf,
I would give you back yourself,
And power to discriminate
What you want and want it not too late,
Many fair days free from care
And heart to enjoy both foul and fair,
And myself, too, if I could find
Where it lay hidden and it proved kind.

Digging

To-day I think
Only with scents,—scents dead leaves yield,
And bracken, and wild carrot's seed,
And the square mustard field;

Odours that rise
When the spade wounds the root of tree,
Rose, currant, raspberry, or goutweed,
Rhubarb or celery;

The smoke's smell, too,
Flowing from where a bonfire burns
The dead, the waste, the dangerous,
And all to sweetness turns.

It is enough
To smell, to crumble the dark earth,
While the robin sings over again
Sad songs of Autumn mirth.

Sowing

It was a perfect day
For sowing; just
As sweet and dry was the ground
As tobacco-dust.

I tasted deep the hour
Between the far
Owl's chuckling first soft cry
And the first star.

A long stretched hour it was;
Nothing undone
Remained; the early seeds
All safely sown.

And now, hark at the rain,
Windless and light,
Half a kiss, half a tear,
Saying good-night.

Tall Nettles

Tall nettles cover up, as they have done
These many springs, the rusty harrow, the plough
Long worn out, and the roller made of stone:
Only the elm butt tops the nettles now.

This corner of the farmyard I like most:
As well as any bloom upon a flower
I like the dust on the nettles, never lost
Except to prove the sweetness of a shower.

The Cherry Trees

The cherry trees bend over and are shedding,
On the old road where all that passed are dead,
Their petals, strewing the grass as for a wedding
This early May morn when there is none to wed.

But These Things Also

But these things also are Spring's—
On banks by the roadside the grass
Long-dead that is greyer now
Than all the Winter it was;

The shell of a little snail bleached
In the grass; chip of flint, and mite
Of chalk; and the small birds' dung
In splashes of purest white:

All the white things a man mistakes
For earliest violets
Who seeks through Winter's ruins
Something to pay Winter's debts,

While the North blows, and starling flocks
By chattering on and on
Keep their spirits up in the mist,
And Spring's here, Winter's not gone.

March the Third[1]

Here again (she said) is March the third
And twelve hours' singing for the bird
'Twixt dawn and dusk, from half-past six
To half-past six, never unheard.

'Tis Sunday, and the church-bells end
When the birds do. I think they blend
Now better than they will when passed
In this unnamed, unmarked godsend.

Or do all mark, and none dares say,
How it may shift and long delay,
Somewhere before the first of Spring,
But never fails, this singing day?

[1] The Author's Birthday

44

And when it falls on Sunday, bells
Are a wild natural voice that dwells
On hillsides; but the birds' songs have
The holiness gone from the bells.

This day unpromised is more dear
Than all the named days of the year
When seasonable sweets come in,
Because we know how lucky we are.

The Child on the Cliffs

Mother, the root of this little yellow flower
Among the stones has the taste of quinine.
Things are strange to-day on the cliff. The sun shines so
    bright,
And the grasshopper works at his sewing-machine
So hard. Here's one on my hand, mother, look;
I lie so still. There's one on your book.

But I have something to tell more strange. So leave
Your book to the grasshopper, mother dear,—
Like a green knight in a dazzling market-place,—
And listen now. Can you hear what I hear
Far out? Now and then the foam there curls
And stretches a white arm out like a girl's.

Fishes and gulls ring no bells. There cannot be
A chapel or church between here and Devon,
With fishes or gulls ringing its bell,—hark!—
Somewhere under the sea or up in heaven.
'It's the bell, my son, out in the bay
On the buoy. It does sound sweet to-day.'

Sweeter I never heard, mother, no, not in all Wales.
I should like to be lying under that foam,
Dead, but able to hear the sound of the bell,
And certain that you would often come
And rest, listening happily.
I should be happy if that could be.

The Child in the Orchard

'He rolls in the orchard: he is stained with moss
And with earth, the solitary old white horse.
Where is his father and where is his mother
Among all the brown horses? Has he a brother?
I know the swallow, the hawk, and the hern;
But there are two million things for me to learn.

'Who was the lady that rode the white horse
With rings and bells to Banbury Cross?
Was there no other lady in England beside
That a nursery rhyme could take for a ride?
The swift, the swallow, the hawk, and the hern.
There are two million things for me to learn.

'Was there a man once who straddled across
The back of the Westbury White Horse
Over there on Salisbury Plain's green wall?
Was he bound for Westbury, or had he a fall?
The swift, the swallow, the hawk, and the hern.
There are two million things for me to learn.

'Out of all the white horses I know three,
At the age of six; and it seems to me
There is so much to learn, for men,
That I dare not go to bed again.
The swift, the swallow, the hawk, and the hern.
There are millions of things for me to learn.'

The Wasp Trap

This moonlight makes
The lovely lovelier
Than ever before lakes
And meadows were.

And yet they are not,
Though this their hour is, more
Lovely than things that were not
Lovely before.

Nothing on earth,
And in the heavens no star,
For pure brightness is worth
More than that jar,

For wasps meant, now
A star—long may it swing
From the dead apple-bough,
So glistening.

Adlestrop

Yes. I remember Adlestrop—
The name, because one afternoon
Of heat the express-train drew up there
Unwontedly. It was late June.

The steam hissed. Someone cleared his throat.
No one left and no one came
On the bare platform. What I saw
Was Adlestrop—only the name

And willows, willow-herb, and grass,
And meadowsweet, and haycocks dry,
No whit less still and lonely fair
Than the high cloudlets in the sky.

And for that minute a blackbird sang
Close by, and round him, mistier,
Farther and farther, all the birds
Of Oxfordshire and Gloucestershire.

Two Pewits

Under the after-sunset sky
Two pewits sport and cry,
More white than is the moon on high
Riding the dark surge silently;
More black than earth. Their cry
Is the one sound under the sky.
They alone move, now low, now high,
And merrily they cry
To the mischievous Spring sky,
Plunging earthward, tossing high,
Over the ghost who wonders why
So merrily they cry and fly,
Nor choose 'twixt earth and sky,
While the moon's quarter silently
Rides, and earth rests as silently.

The Path

Running along a bank, a parapet
That saves from the precipitous wood below
The level road, there is a path. It serves
Children for looking down the long smooth steep,
Between the legs of beech and yew, to where
A fallen tree checks the sight: while men and women
Content themselves with the road and what they see
Over the bank, and what the children tell.
The path, winding like silver, trickles on,
Bordered and even invaded by thinnest moss
That tries to cover roots and crumbling chalk
With gold, olive, and emerald, but in vain.
The children wear it. They have flattened the bank
On top, and silvered it between the moss
With the current of their feet, year after year.
But the road is houseless, and leads not to school.
To see a child is rare there, and the eye
Has but the road, the wood that overhangs
And underyawns it, and the path that looks
As if it led on to some legendary
Or fancied place where men have wished to go
And stay; till, sudden, it ends where the wood ends.

The Owl

Downhill I came, hungry, and yet not starved;
Cold, yet had heat within me that was proof
Against the North wind; tired, yet so that rest
Had seemed the sweetest thing under a roof.

Then at the inn I had food, fire, and rest,
Knowing how hungry, cold, and tired was I.
All of the night was quite barred out except
An owl's cry, a most melancholy cry

Shaken out long and clear upon the hill,
No merry note, nor cause of merriment,
But one telling me plain what I escaped
And others could not, that night, as in I went.

And salted was my food, and my repose,
Salted and sobered, too, by the bird's voice
Speaking for all who lay under the stars,
Soldiers and poor, unable to rejoice.

A Cat

She had a name among the children;
But no one loved though someone owned
Her, locked her out of doors at bedtime
And had her kittens duly drowned.

In Spring, nevertheless, this cat
Ate blackbirds, thrushes, nightingales,
And birds of bright voice and plume and flight,
As well as scraps from neighbours' pails.

I loathed and hated her for this;
One speckle on a thrush's breast
Was worth a million such; and yet
She lived long, till God gave her rest.

The Combe

The Combe was ever dark, ancient and dark.
Its mouth is stopped with bramble, thorn, and briar;
And no one scrambles over the sliding chalk
By beech and yew and perishing juniper
Down the half precipices of its sides, with roots
And rabbit holes for steps. The sun of Winter,
The moon of Summer, and all the singing birds
Except the missel-thrush that loves juniper,
Are quite shut out. But far more ancient and dark
The Combe looks since they killed the badger there,
Dug him out and gave him to the hounds,
That most ancient Briton of English beasts.

The Dark Forest

Dark is the forest and deep, and overhead
Hang stars like seeds of light
In vain, though not since they were sown was bred
Anything more bright.

And evermore mighty multitudes ride
About, nor enter in;
Of the other multitudes that dwell inside
Never yet was one seen.

The forest foxglove is purple, the marguerite
Outside is gold and white,
Nor can those that pluck either blossom greet
The others, day or night.

The Gallows

There was a weasel lived in the sun
With all his family,
Till a keeper shot him with his gun
And hung him up on a tree,
Where he swings in the wind and rain,
In the sun and in the snow,
Without pleasure, without pain,
On the dead oak tree bough.

There was a crow who was no sleeper,
But a thief and a murderer
Till a very late hour; and this keeper
Made him one of the things that were,
To hang and flap in rain and wind,
In the sun and in the snow.
There are no more sins to be sinned
On the dead oak tree bough.

There was a magpie, too,
Had a long tongue and a long tail;
He could both talk and do—
But what did that avail?
He, too, flaps in the wind and rain
Alongside weasel and crow,
Without pleasure, without pain,
On the dead oak tree bough.

And many other beasts
And birds, skin, bone, and feather,
Have been taken from their feasts
And hung up there together,
To swing and have endless leisure
In the sun and in the snow,
Without pain, without pleasure,
On the dead oak tree bough.

The Lofty Sky

To-day I want the sky,
The tops of the high hills,
Above the last man's house,
His hedges, and his cows,
Where, if I will, I look
Down even on sheep and rook,
And of all things that move
See buzzards only above:—
Past all trees, past furze
And thorn, where nought deters
The desire of the eye
For sky, nothing but sky.

I sicken of the woods
And all the multitudes
Of hedge-trees. They are no more
Than weeds upon this floor
Of the river of air
Leagues deep, leagues wide, where
I am like a fish that lives
In weeds and mud and gives
What's above him no thought.
I might be a tench for aught
That I can do to-day
Down on the wealden clay.
Even the tench has days
When he floats up and plays
Among the lily leaves
And sees the sky, or grieves
Not if he nothing sees:
While I, I know that trees
Under that lofty sky
Are weeds, fields, mud, and I
Would arise and go far
To where the lilies are.

Aspens

All day and night, save winter, every weather,
Above the inn, the smithy, and the shop,
The aspens at the cross-roads talk together
Of rain, until their last leaves fall from the top.

Out of the blacksmith's cavern comes the ringing
Of hammer, shoe, and anvil; out of the inn
The clink, the hum, the roar, the random singing—
The sounds that for these fifty years have been.

The whisper of the aspens is not drowned,
And over lightless pane and footless road,
Empty as sky, with every other sound
Not ceasing, calls their ghosts from their abode,

A silent smithy, a silent inn, nor fails
In the bare moonlight or the thick-furred gloom,
In tempest or the night of nightingales,
To turn the cross-roads to a ghostly room.

And it would be the same were no house near.
Over all sorts of weather, men, and times,
Aspens must shake their leaves and men may hear
But need not listen, more than to my rhymes.

Whatever wind blows, while they and I have leaves
We cannot other than an aspen be
That ceaselessly, unreasonably grieves,
Or so men think who like a different tree.

The Mill-Water

Only the sound remains
Of the old mill;
Gone is the wheel;
On the prone roof and walls the nettle reigns.

Water that toils no more
Dangles white locks
And, falling, mocks
The music of the mill-wheel's busy roar.

Pretty to see, by day
Its sound is naught
Compared with thought
And talk and noise of labour and of play.

Night makes the difference.
In calm moonlight,
Gloom infinite,
The sound comes surging in upon the sense:

Solitude, company,—
When it is night,—
Grief or delight
By it must haunted or concluded be.

Often the silentness
Has but this one
Companion;
Wherever one creeps in the other is:

Sometimes a thought is drowned
By it, sometimes
Out of it climbs;
All thoughts begin or end upon this sound,

Only the idle foam
Of water falling
Changelessly calling,
Where once men had a work-place and a home.

After Rain

The rain of a night and a day and a night
Stops at the light
Of this pale choked day. The peering sun
Sees what has been done.
The road under the trees has a border new
Of purple hue
Inside the border of bright thin grass:
For all that has
Been left by November of leaves is torn
From hazel and thorn
And the greater trees. Throughout the copse
No dead leaf drops
On grey grass, green moss, burnt-orange fern,
At the wind's return:
The leaflets out of the ash-tree shed
Are thinly spread
In the road, like little black fish, inlaid,
As if they played.

What hangs from the myriad branches down there
So hard and bare
Is twelve yellow apples lovely to see
On one crab-tree.
And on each twig of every tree in the dell
Uncountable
Crystals both dark and bright of the rain
That begins again.

October

The green elm with the one great bough of gold
Lets leaves into the grass slip, one by one,—
The short hill grass, the mushrooms small, milk-white,
Harebell and scabious and tormentil,
That blackberry and gorse, in dew and sun,
Bow down to; and the wind travels too light
To shake the fallen birch leaves from the fern;
The gossamers wander at their own will.
At heavier steps than birds' the squirrels scold.
The rich scene has grown fresh again and new
As Spring and to the touch is not more cool
Than it is warm to the gaze; and now I might
As happy be as earth is beautiful,
Were I some other or with earth could turn
In alternation of violet and rose,
Harebell and snowdrop, at their season due,
And gorse that has no time not to be gay.
But if this be not happiness,—who knows?
Some day I shall think this a happy day,
And this mood by the name of melancholy
Shall no more blackened and obscurèd be.

November

November's days are thirty:
November's earth is dirty,
Those thirty days, from first to last;
And the prettiest things on ground are the paths
With morning and evening hobnails dinted,
With foot and wing-tip overprinted
Or separately charactered,
Of little beast and little bird.
The fields are mashed by sheep, the roads
Make the worst going, the best the woods
Where dead leaves upward and downward scatter.
Few care for the mixture of earth and water,
Twig, leaf, flint, thorn,
Straw, feather, all that men scorn,
Pounded up and sodden by flood,
Condemned as mud.

But of all the months when earth is greener
Not one has clean skies that are cleaner.
Clean and clear and sweet and cold,
They shine above the earth so old,
While the after-tempest cloud
Sails over in silence though winds are loud,
Till the full moon in the east
Looks at the planet in the west
And earth is silent as it is black,
Yet not unhappy for its lack.
Up from the dirty earth men stare:
One imagines a refuge there
Above the mud, in the pure bright
Of the cloudless heavenly light:
Another loves earth and November more dearly
Because without them, he sees clearly,
The sky would be nothing more to his eye
Than he, in any case, is to the sky;
He loves even the mud whose dyes
Renounce all brightness to the skies.

There's Nothing Like the Sun

There's nothing like the sun as the year dies,
Kind as it can be, this world being made so,
To stones and men and beasts and birds and flies,
To all things that it touches except snow,
Whether on mountain side or street of town.
The south wall warms me: November has begun,
Yet never shone the sun as fair as now
While the sweet last-left damsons from the bough
With spangles of the morning's storm drop down
Because the starling shakes it, whistling what
Once swallows sang. But I have not forgot
That there is nothing, too, like March's sun,
Like April's, or July's, or June's, or May's,
Or January's, or February's, great days:

August, September, October, and December
Have equal days, all different from November.
No day of any month but I have said—
Or, if I could live long enough, should say—
'There's nothing like the sun that shines to-day.'
There's nothing like the sun till we are dead.

Fifty Faggots

There they stand, on their ends, the fifty faggots
That once were underwood of hazel and ash
In Jenny Pinks's Copse. Now, by the hedge
Close packed, they make a thicket fancy alone
Can creep through with the mouse and wren. Next Spring
A blackbird or a robin will nest there,
Accustomed to them, thinking they will remain
Whatever is for ever to a bird:

This Spring it is too late; the swift has come.
'Twas a hot day for carrying them up:
Better they will never warm me, though they must
Light several Winters' fires. Before they are done
The war will have ended, many other things
Have ended, maybe, that I can no more
Foresee or more control than robin and wren.

Snow

In the gloom of whiteness,
In the great silence of snow,
A child was sighing
And bitterly saying: 'Oh,
They have killed a white bird up there on her nest,
The down is fluttering from her breast!'
And still it fell through that dusky brightness
On the child crying for the bird of the snow.

Thaw

Over the land freckled with snow half-thawed
The speculating rooks at their nests cawed
And saw from elm-tops, delicate as flower of grass,
What we below could not see, Winter pass.

Roads

I love roads:
The goddesses that dwell
Far along invisible
Are my favourite gods.

Roads go on
While we forget, and are
Forgotten like a star
That shoots and is gone.

On this earth 'tis sure
We men have not made
Anything that doth fade
So soon, so long endure:

The hill road wet with rain
In the sun would not gleam
Like a winding stream
If we trod it not again.

They are lonely
While we sleep, lonelier
For lack of the traveller
Who is now a dream only.

From dawn's twilight
And all the clouds like sheep
On the mountains of sleep
They wind into the night.

The next turn may reveal
Heaven: upon the crest
The close pine clump, at rest
And black, may Hell conceal.

Often footsore, never
Yet of the road I weary,
Though long and steep and dreary,
As it winds on for ever.

Helen of the roads,
The mountain ways of Wales
And the Mabinogion tales
Is one of the true gods,

Abiding in the trees,
The threes and fours so wise,
The larger companies,
That by the roadside be,

And beneath the rafter
Else uninhabited
Excepting by the dead;
And it is her laughter

At morn and night I hear
When the thrush cock sings
Bright irrelevant things
And when the chanticleer

Calls back to their own night
Troops that make loneliness
With their light footsteps' press,
As Helen's own are light.

Now all roads lead to France
And heavy is the tread
Of the living; but the dead
Returning lightly dance:

Whatever the roads bring
To me or take from me,
They keep me company
With their pattering,

Crowding the solitude
Of the loops over the downs,
Hushing the roar of towns
And their brief multitude.

Two

Two

The Penny Whistle

The new moon hangs like an ivory bugle
In the naked frosty blue;
And the ghylls of the forest, already blackened
By Winter, are blackened anew.

The brooks that cut up and increase the forest,
As if they had never known
The sun, are roaring with black hollow voices
Betwixt rage and a moan.

But still the caravan-hut by the hollies
Like a kingfisher gleams between:
Round the mossed old hearths of the charcoal-burners
First primroses ask to be seen.

The charcoal-burners are black, but their linen
Blows white on the line;
And white the letter the girl is reading
Under that crescent fine;

And her brother who hides apart in a thicket,
Slowly and surely playing
On a whistle an old nursery melody
Says far more than I am saying.

An Old Song

I was not apprenticed nor ever dwelt in famous Lincoln-
    shire;
I've served one master ill and well much more than seven
    year;
And never took up to poaching as you shall quickly find;
   But 'tis my delight of a shiny night in the season of the
    year.

I roamed where nobody had a right but keepers and
    squires, and there
I sought for nests, wild flowers, oak sticks, and moles, both
    far and near.
And had to run from farmers, and learnt the Lincolnshire
    song:
   'Oh, 'tis my delight of a shiny night in the season of the
    year.'

I took those walks years after, talking with friend or dear,
Or solitary musing; but when the moon shone clear
I had no joy or sorrow that could not be expressed
   By ' 'Tis my delight of a shiny night in the season of the
    year.'

Since then I've thrown away a chance to fight a game-
keeper;
And I less often trespass, and what I see or hear
Is mostly from the road or path by day: yet still I sing:
   'Oh, 'tis my delight of a shiny night in the season of the
   year.'

For if I am contented, at home or anywhere,
Or if I sigh for I know not what, or my heart beats with
some fear,
It is a strange kind of delight to sing or whistle just:
   'Oh, 'tis my delight of a shiny night in the season of the
   year.'

And with this melody on my lips and no one by to care,
Indoors, or out on shiny nights or dark in open air,
I am for a moment made a man that sings out of his heart:
   'Oh, 'tis my delight of a shiny night in the season of the
   year.'

Will You Come?

Will you come?
Will you come?
Will you ride
So late
At my side?
O, will you come?

Will you come?
Will you come
If the night
Has a moon
Full and bright?
O, will you come?

Would you come?
Would you come
If the noon
Gave light,
Not the moon?
Beautiful, would you come?

Would you have come?
Would you have come
Without scorning,
Had it been
Still morning?
Beloved, would you have come?

If you come
Haste and come.
Owls have cried;
It grows dark
To ride.
Beloved, beautiful, come.

Song

At poet's tears,
Sweeter than any smiles but hers,
She laughs; I sigh;
And yet I could not live if she should die.

And when in June
Once more the cuckoo spoils his tune,
She laughs at sighs;
And yet she says she loves me till she dies.

The Clouds That Are So Light

As the clouds that are so light,
Beautiful, swift, and bright,
Cast shadows on field and park
Of the earth that is so dark,

And even so now, light one!
Beautiful, swift and bright one!
You let fall on a heart that was dark,
Unillumined, a deeper mark.

But clouds would have, without earth
To shadow, far less worth:
Away from your shadow on me
Your beauty less would be,

And if it still be treasured
An age hence, it shall be measured
By this small dark spot
Without which it were not.

An Old Song

The sun set, the wind fell, the sea
Was like a mirror shaking:
The one small wave that clapped the land
A mile-long snake of foam was making
Where tide had smoothed and wind had dried
The vacant sand.

A light divided the swollen clouds
And lay most perfectly
Like a straight narrow footbridge bright
That crossed over the sea to me;
And no one else in the whole world
Saw that same sight.

I walked elate, my bridge always
Just one step from my feet:
A robin sang, a shade in shade:
And all I did was to repeat:
'I'll go no more a-roving
With you, fair maid.'

The sailors' song of merry loving
With dusk and sea-gull's mewing
Mixed sweet, the lewdness far outweighed
By the wild charm the chorus played:
'I'll go no more a-roving
With you, fair maid:
A-roving, a-roving, since roving's been my ruin,
I'll go no more a-roving with you, fair maid.'

In Amsterdam there dwelt a maid—
Mark well what I do say—
In Amsterdam there dwelt a maid
And she was a mistress of her trade:
I'll go no more a-roving
With you, fair maid:
A-roving, a-roving, since roving's been my ruin,
I'll go no more a-roving with you, fair maid.

Three

Interval

Gone the wild day:
A wilder night
Coming makes way
For brief twilight.

Where the firm soaked road
Mounts and is lost
In the high beech-wood
It shines almost.

The beeches keep
A stormy rest,
Breathing deep
Of wind from the west.

The wood is black,
With a misty steam.
Above, the cloud pack
Breaks for one gleam.

But the woodman's cot
By the ivied trees
Awakens not
To light or breeze.

It smokes aloft
Unwavering:
It hunches soft
Under storm's wing.

It has no care
For gleam or gloom:
It stays there
While I shall roam,

Die, and forget
The hill of trees,
The gleam, the wet,
This roaring peace.

Out in the Dark

Out in the dark over the snow
The fallow fawns invisible go
With the fallow doe;
And the winds blow
Fast as the stars are slow.

Stealthily the dark haunts round
And, when the lamp goes, without sound
At a swifter bound
Than the swiftest hound,
Arrives, and all else is drowned;

And star and I and wind and deer,
Are in the dark together,—near,
Yet far,—and fear
Drums on my ear
In that sage company drear.

How weak and little is the light,
All the universe of sight,
Love and delight,
Before the might,
If you love it not, of night.

Gone, Gone Again

Gone, gone again,
May, June, July,
And August gone,
Again gone by.

Not memorable
Save that I saw them go,
As past the empty quays
The rivers flow.

And now again,
In the harvest rain,
The Blenheim oranges
Fall grubby from the trees

As when I was young—
And when the lost one was here—
And when the war began
To turn young men to dung.

Look at the old house,
Outmoded, dignified,
Dark and untenanted,
With grass growing instead

Of the footsteps of life,
The friendliness, the strife;
In its beds have lain
Youth, love, age, and pain:

I am something like that;
Only I am not dead,
Still breathing and interested
In the house that is not dark:—

I am something like that:
Not one pane to reflect the sun,
For the schoolboys to throw at—
They have broken every one.

The Long Small Room

The long small room that showed willows in the west
Narrowed up to the end the fireplace filled,
Although not wide. I liked it. No one guessed
What need or accident made them so build.

Only the moon, the mouse and the sparrow peeped
In from the ivy round the casement thick.
Of all they saw and heard there they shall keep
The tale for the old ivy and older brick.

When I look back I am like moon, sparrow, and mouse
That witnessed what they could never understand
Or alter or prevent in the dark house.
One thing remains the same—this my right hand

Crawling crab-like over the clean white page,
Resting awhile each morning on the pillow,
Then once more starting to crawl on towards age.
The hundred last leaves stream upon the willow.

Home

Not the end: but there's nothing more.
Sweet Summer and Winter rude
I have loved, and friendship and love,
The crowd and solitude:

But I know them: I weary not;
But all that they mean I know.
I would go back again home
Now. Yet how should I go?

This is my grief. That land,
My home, I have never seen;
No traveller tells of it,
However far he has been.

And could I discover it,
I fear my happiness there,
Or my pain, might be dreams of return
Here, to these things that were.

Remembering ills, though slight
Yet irremediable,
Brings a worse, an impurer pang
Than remembering what was well.

No: I cannot go back,
And would not if I could.
Until blindness come, I must wait
And blink at what is not good.

Beauty

What does it mean? Tired, angry, and ill at ease,
No man, woman, or child alive could please
Me now. And yet I almost dare to laugh
Because I sit and frame an epitaph—
'Here lies all that no one loved of him
And that loved no one.' Then in a trice that whim
Has wearied. But, though I am like a river
At fall of evening while it seems that never
Has the sun lighted it or warmed it, while
Cross breezes cut the surface to a file,
This heart, some fraction of me, happily
Floats through the window even now to a tree

Down in the misting, dim-lit, quiet vale,
Not like a pewit that returns to wail
For something it has lost, but like a dove
That slants unswerving to its home and love.
There I find my rest, and through the dusk air
Flies what yet lives in me. Beauty is there.

The Glory

The glory of the beauty of the morning,—
The cuckoo crying over the untouched dew;
The blackbird that has found it, and the dove
That tempts me on to something sweeter than love;
White clouds ranged even and fair as new-mown hay;
The heat, the stir, the sublime vacancy
Of sky and meadow and forest and my own heart:—
The glory invites me, yet it leaves me scorning
All I can ever do, all I can be,
Beside the lovely of motion, shape, and hue,
The happiness I fancy fit to dwell
In beauty's presence. Shall I now this day
Begin to seek as far as heaven, as hell,
Wisdom or strength to match this beauty, start
And tread the pale dust pitted with small dark drops,
In hope to find whatever it is I seek,

Hearkening to short-lived happy-seeming things
That we know naught of, in the hazel copse?
Or must I be content with discontent
As larks and swallows are perhaps with wings?
And shall I ask at the day's end once more
What beauty is, and what I can have meant
By happiness? And shall I let all go,
Glad, weary, or both? Or shall I perhaps know
That I was happy oft and oft before,
Awhile forgetting how I am fast pent,
How dreary-swift, with naught to travel to,
Is Time? I cannot bite the day to the core.

Four

Four

The Trumpet

Rise up, rise up,
And, as the trumpet blowing
Chases the dreams of men,
As the dawn glowing
The stars that left unlit
The land and water,
Rise up and scatter
The dew that covers
The print of last night's lovers—
Scatter it, scatter it!

While you are listening
To the clear horn,
Forget, men, everything
On this earth new-born,
Except that it is lovelier
Than any mysteries.
Open your eyes to the air
That has washed the eyes of the stars
Through all the dewy night:
Up with the light,
To the old wars;
Arise, arise!

This is No Case of
Petty Right or Wrong

This is no case of petty right or wrong
That politicians or philosophers
Can judge. I hate not Germans, nor grow hot
With love of Englishmen, to please newspapers.
Beside my hate for one fat patriot
My hatred of the Kaiser is love true:—
A kind of god he is, banging a gong.
But I have not to choose between the two,
Or between justice and injustice. Dinned
With war and argument I read no more

Than in the storm smoking along the wind
Athwart the wood. Two witches' cauldrons roar.
From one the weather shall rise clear and gay;
Out of the other an England beautiful
And like her mother that died yesterday.
Little I know or care if, being dull,
I shall miss something that historians
Can rake out of the ashes when perchance
The phoenix broods serene above their ken.
But with the best and meanest Englishmen
I am one in crying, God save England, lest
We lose what never slaves and cattle blessed.
The ages made her that made us from dust:
She is all we know and live by, and we trust
She is good and must endure, loving her so:
And as we love ourselves we hate her foe.

No One Cares Less than I

'No one cares less than I,
Nobody knows but God,
Whether I am destined to lie
Under a foreign clod,'
Were the words I made to the bugle call in the morning.

But laughing, storming, scorning,
Only the bugles know
What the bugles say in the morning,
And they do not care, when they blow
The call that I heard and made words to early this morning.

Early One Morning

Early one morning in May I set out,
And nobody I knew was about.
    I'm bound away for ever,
      Away somewhere, away for ever.

There was no wind to trouble the weathercocks.
I had burnt my letters and darned my socks.

No one knew I was going away,
I thought myself I should come back some day.

I heard the brook through the town gardens run.
O sweet was the mud turned to dust by the sun.

A gate banged in a fence and banged in my head.
'A fine morning, sir,' a shepherd said.

I could not return from my liberty,
To my youth and my love and my misery.

The past is the only dead thing that smells sweet,
The only sweet thing that is not also fleet.
    I'm bound away for ever,
      Away somewhere, away for ever.

Lights Out

I have come to the borders of sleep,
The unfathomable deep
Forest where all must lose
Their way, however straight,
Or winding, soon or late;
They cannot choose.

Many a road and track
That, since the dawn's first crack,
Up to the forest brink,
Deceived the travellers,
Suddenly now blurs,
And in they sink.

Here love ends,
Despair, ambition ends;
All pleasure and all trouble,
Although most sweet or bitter,
Here ends in sleep that is sweeter
Than tasks most noble.

There is not any book
Or face of dearest look
That I would not turn from now
To go into the unknown
I must enter, and leave, alone,
I know not how.

The tall forest towers;
Its cloudy foliage lowers
Ahead, shelf above shelf;
Its silence I hear and obey
That I may lose my way
And myself.

In Memoriam (Easter, 1915)

The flowers left thick at nightfall in the wood
This Eastertide call into mind the men,
Now far from home, who, with their sweethearts, should
Have gathered them and will do never again.

Five

Words

Out of us all
That make rhymes,
Will you choose
Sometimes—
As the winds use
A crack in a wall
Or a drain,
Their joy or their pain
To whistle through—
Choose me,
You English words?

I know you:
You are light as dreams,
Tough as oak,
Precious as gold,
As poppies and corn,
Or an old cloak:
Sweet as our birds
To the ear,
As the burnet rose
In the heat
Of Midsummer:

Strange as the races
Of dead and unborn:
Strange and sweet
Equally,
And familiar,
To the eye,
As the dearest faces
That a man knows,
And as lost homes are:
But though older far
Than oldest yew,—
As our hills are, old,—
Worn new
Again and again:
Young as our streams
After rain:
And as dear
As the earth which you prove
That we love.

Make me content
With some sweetness
From Wales
Whose nightingales
Have no wings,—
From Wiltshire and Kent
And Herefordshire,

And the villages there,—
From the names, and the things
No less.
Let me sometimes dance
With you,
Or climb
Or stand perchance
In ecstasy,
Fixed and free
In a rhyme,
As poets do.

Title Index

Index of First Lines

It was EDWARD THOMAS, as a literary critic, who brought the poetry of his close friend, Robert Frost, to the attention of the British public—and it was Robert Frost who first perceived Thomas's extraordinary sensitivity to experience and to the expression of words and who urged him to write poetry.

Thomas's tragic death on a battlefield of World War I came only two years after he began writing poetry—and he never lived to see his poems in print. But the legacy he left to literature, however small in quantity by its untimely end, was great and significant in its quality and established him as one of England's foremost poets.

ELEANOR FARJEON, a distinguished woman of letters and one of the most famous and respected of children's book authors both here and in England, like Robert Frost, recognized the promise of her close friend, Edward Thomas, as a poet. Her great admiration of his work and of Thomas himself led to her selection of some of his poems for young readers, and for them she has written a moving Foreword, describing Thomas as she knew him for those "to whom Edward Thomas has never been a living personality." Her perceptive observations of his life and his work take on particular meaning in light of Miss Farjeon's own untimely death, shortly after completion of her work on this book, which she will never see in print.